CW00684003

LATANOPROST VARIATIONS

LATANOPROST VARIATIONS

JEFF HILSON

BOILER HOUSE PRESS

ONE

TWO

THREE FOUR FIVE

ONCE

SLATES 1 & 2

A great many think that they know repetition when they see or hear it but do they.

— Gertrude Stein, 'Portraits and Repetition'

Keep this book. You may need to read it again. Do not pass it on to others. It may harm them, even if their signs of illness are the same as yours.

— Latanoprost 50 Micrograms/ml Eye drops, solution

then i realised we werent in england
but in a british movie.

— piero heliczer, 'england'

ONE

people who listen to marvin gaye are also listening to
perry como since you listened to marvin gaye you might
liken this new release by bing crosby if you listened to
the kinks heres an album you might not liken if you
liken the kinks try the cure if you liken marvin gaye we
recommend dean martin you listened to the talking
heads check out caravan you listened to boards of canada
and aphex twins heres an album you might not liken
since you listened to the talking heads you might liken
this new release by comus people who listen to the kinks
are also listening to the nice you listened to the talking
heads and aphex twins heres an album you might not
liken people who listen to the feelies are also listening to
the ghoulies you listened to gang of four and boards of
canada heres an album you might not liken you listened
to throbbing gristle heres a song you might not liken if
you liken supertramp try henry cow since you listened to
prince far I you might liken this new release by egg you
listened to kate bush and the talking heads check out the
alan parsons project if you liken talk talk we recommend

quiet sun you listened to the feelies check out the ghoulies you listened to supertramp heres an album you might not liken since you listened to throbbing gristle check out simon and garfunkel if you liken gang of four try the only ones you listened to prince far I heres a song you might not liken you listened to swell maps this week liken to try the wilde flowers? since you listened to the kinks you might liken the fall you listened to talk talk heres a song you might not liken you listened to gang of four try MC5 liken boards of canada and aphex twins? check out lol coxhill people who listen to the kinks are also listening to the band you listened to sparks heres an album you might not liken if you liken gang of four try 999 people who listen to supertramp are also listening to elton dean if you liken prince far I we recommend mom you listened to marvin gaye heres an album you might not liken since you listened to the feelies check out the ghoulies you listened to john butt try marga hoffgen you listened to the talking heads check out the matching mole people who listen to the incredible string band are also listening to the matching mole you listened to john butt this week try das orchester der bayreuther festspiele you listened to talk talk heres an album you might not liken if you liken the feelies we recommend the ghoulies you listened to kate bush heres an album you might not liken you listened to the feelies you might not liken this song people who listen to prince far I are also listening to gong if you liken gang of four we recommend S club 7 you listened to prince far I heres a song you might not liken you listened to the talking heads check out amoeba split you listened to the feelies you might not liken this song you listened to talk talk check out quiet sun you listened to the incredible string band heres an album you might not liken if you liken the incredible string band try audience if you liken marvin gaye try van morrison you listened to the talking heads heres an album you might not liken people who listen to sparks are also listening to van dyke parks you listened to marvin gaye heres an album you might not liken you listened to throbbing gristle you might not liken this song if you liken the talking heads try national health people who listen to prince far I are also listening to cos if you liken the incredible string band we recommend the soft machine you listened to swell maps this week liken to try the wilde flowers? you listened to kate bush check out kevin ayers if you liken marvin gaye try gavin bryers you listened to the incredible string band check out dr strangely strange you listened to prince far I heres an album you might not liken people who listen to the incredible string band are also listening to the bonzo dog band you listened to john butt this week try angelika kirchschlager you listened to gang of four heres an album you might not liken if you liken aphex twins we recommend pip pyles you listened to gang of four check out three dog night you listened to gang of four heres an album you might not liken you listened to kate bush check out kevin coyne if you liken prince far I try khan you listened to boards of canada and aphex twins heres an album you might not liken people who listen to aphex twins are also listening to pip pyles if you liken the incredible string band try hatfield and the north you listened to aphex twins heres an album you might not liken you listened to supertramp and kate bush you might not liken this song you listened to swell maps this week liken to try the wilde flowers? if you liken boards of canada we recommend caravan of dreams if you liken talk talk try quiet sun you listened to the incredible string band check out rare bird you listened to boards of canada and aphex twins check out lol coxhill you listened to john butt this week try dagmar krause you listened to swell maps this week liken to try again the wilde flowers? you listened to marvin gaye this week liken to try again perry como? you listened to the talking heads this week liken to try again the matching mole?

See how Sunny compares.
  — sunny.co.uk

now we are in a wogan economy wogan is always lending me money its quite simple in a minute wogan will contact me & with my wogan money I will buy a white knight condenser tumble dryer thanks wogan I am always recommending you to my friends I love to borrow money from wogan dont have a kindle? its quite simple in a minute wogan will contact me & I will buy a small brown suede effect ottoman I love to borrow money from wogan because wogan is my favourite lender with my wogan money I will buy a babyliss essential bikini trimmer I dont think I will buy a discovery channel digital metal detector now we are in the wogan economy I will buy a hostess retro portable silver food warmer I dont think I will buy a varta indestructible L-E-D torch wogan is my favourite lender he asks me how much money I want thanks wogan I am always recommending you to my friends dont have a kindle? its quite simple in a minute wogan will contact me & I will buy an indesit silver undercounter fridge I dont think I will buy an aerolatte stainless steel milk frother I feel well informed by wogan he is always lending me money I agree his service is easy to use I can always change my mind look I just bought a discovery channel digital metal detector I didnt buy a white knight condenser tumble dryer I swear I would be lost if I didnt have wogan wogan is always lending me money its quite simple in a minute wogan will contact me & with my wogan money I will buy a sentry jumbo fire & waterproof safe dont have a kindle? its quite simple in a minute wogan will contact me I cant see what the problem is I love to borrow money from wogan wogan is my favourite lender with my wogan money I will buy a challenge xtreme orbital sander thanks wogan I am always recommending you to my friends its quite simple I will buy a challenge xtreme impact garden shredder because wogan is my favourite lender everyone knows what their getting into I cant see what the problem is dont have a kindle? its quite simple in a minute wogan will contact me & I will buy a mr & mrs cut out photo frame I will not buy a set of raymond van barnevald super star darts now we are in the wogan economy I can always change my mind look I just bought an aerolatte stainless steel milk frother I didnt buy a small brown suede effect ottoman sometimes I am in a hurry naturally he asks me how much money I want & I buy a partytime by sekonda stoneset watch its quite simple sometimes I am in a hurry & I love to borrow money from wogan wogan is always lending me money thanks wogan I am always recommending you to my friends dont have a kindle? its quite simple in a minute wogan will contact me I cant see what the problem is look I just bought a living antibacterial shower curtain I can safely say I bought a bissel cleanview deep clean carpet cleaner I always turn to wogan he really does what he says he will do its quite simple he says he will lend me money & now we are in the wogan economy I will buy a frost resistant heron pond guard thanks wogan I am always recommending you to my friends because wogan is my favourite lender I can safely say I will buy a white knight condenser tumble dryer I can safely say I will buy a staywell small two way pet door I dont think I will buy a parker high back managers chair dont have a kindle? its quite simple in a minute wogan will contact me I cant see what the problem is everyone knows what their getting into I can always change my mind look I just bought a small brown suede effect ottoman I didnt buy a living antibacterial shower curtain I always turn to wogan he really does what he says he will do its quite simple he says he will lend me money I love to borrow money from wogan wogan is always lending me money now we are in the wogan economy I will buy a davina mccall vinyl dumbbell set I dont think I will buy an oversink kitchen organiser sometimes I am in a hurry he asks me how much money I want & I buy a stylophone pocket electronic organ thanks wogan I am always recommending you to my friends dont have a kindle? its quite simple in a minute wogan will contact me & I will buy a deluxe aluminium self propelled wheelchair I dont think I will buy a no! no! hair classic hair remover now we are in the wogan economy I can always change my mind look I just bought an aerolatte stainless steel milk frother I didnt buy a bissel cleanview deep clean carpet cleaner wogan is crystal clear he urges me to think carefully sometimes I am in a hurry he asks me how much money I want & I buy a david & goliath I love nerds retro messenger bag it is in my best interest to buy a 3 arm freestanding towel rail not a 59 bottle wine chiller it is in my best interest to buy a hygena milan space saver table not a my little pony tilt 'n' turn scooter it is in my best interest to buy a white knight condenser tumble dryer not a celestron powerseeker reflector telescope

Wake up wake up everyone
The day is only dazzling.
  — Lal Waterson, 'Child Among the Weeds'

As I walked out in the morning on the first day looking for the early gentian I didnt find it in the morning instead I found an allis shad did you mean to search for an allis shad & all in the morning on the first day & as I set off in the evening on the second day to seek the creeping marshwort I didnt find it with a lantern instead I found a speckled footman I didnt mean to search for a speckled footman with a lantern or in the evening & taking a turn on the third day in the afternoon I tried to find the three lobed crowfoot I didnt find it instead in the afternoon I found axl rose I was trying to find a three lobed crowfoot instead I found axl rose & I began to cry & as I roved out early one day searching for a slender naiad it was on the fourth day & I didnt find it instead I found a narrow headed ant it was on the fourth day & I didnt find it even though I tried & on the fifth day at sunrise I went abroad looking for a lundy cabbage its just a cabbage I thought &

I didnt find it I couldnt see one anywhere instead in the sun I found a smooth snake I didnt mean to search for & I will surely die & as I strolled along at noon on the sixth day in quest of the western ramping fumitory I didnt find it oh what shall I do instead I found a harbour porpoise & it wasnt the same & as I ventured out at night on the seventh day to locate the holly fern I didnt find it instead I found a slow worm & well the tears fell from me & on the eighth day as I tramped about at dawn on the lookout for a fen orchid I didnt find it instead I found a skylark I didnt mean to search for through the bushes or the briars & I fell down on my knees & as I made my way at sundown in pursuit of a ladys slipper I didnt find one oh it was on the ninth day & instead at midnight with my lily white hands I found a large copper & a cold wind blew through me & on the tenth day as I got going at daybreak to gather in the eyebrights I didnt find any I was blindfolded & instead I found a song thrush did you mean to search for a song thrush for to cut off all its ears & on day eleven at first light as I set off to catch myself a star fruit I didnt find it in the dark instead I found a devils bolete & my heart is in the ground & as I headed out at dusk on the twelfth day to bring in the interrupted brome I didnt find it I found instead a robert plant but it was only make believe & on day thirteen as I left home to pick a plymouth pear unlucky for me I didnt find it I forgot about the time instead & in a ditch I found a glutinous snail I didnt mean to search for no not ever in my life & on the fourteenth day as I sallied forth to locate the norfolk flapwort I didnt find it nor in the light nor in the shade instead I found a grizzled skipper I will never call him captain & as I slipped away on the fifteenth day to uncover the spreading bellflower with the sun overhead I didnt find it instead I found a shrill carder bee I didnt mean to search for & I laughed & I laughed because it sounded just like a robert plant & on day sixteen I arose at dawn to hunt the green hounds tongue & as I did the east was bright I didnt find it instead I found a red backed shrike & as it killed me I cried I'm glad I'm not a red backed shrike & as I made a start at dusk on the seventeenth day to unveil the prickly poppy I didnt I fell asleep & in a dream I found instead the duke of burgundy & oh oh on the kings right knee & on day eighteen as I departed late to flag a deptford pink I didnt find it instead I found a false click beetle a false false thing I didnt mean to search for & on the nineteenth day at twilight as I broke camp to unearth the slender bedstraw I didnt find it instead I found a twinflower & I wished I was whole again & on the twentieth day in the middle of may as I rode out to harvest wild asparagus I didnt find any instead I found a brown hare did you mean to search for a brown hare to take away your language & as I started off on day twenty one to sniff out the stinking goosefoot I didnt find it instead I found a vendace a true white fish I never heard of & though it didnt mean to it too was stinking & as I set forth in good time on the twenty second day to fall upon the ground pine I didnt find it even though I fell upon the ground instead I found a grey dagger & nobody cheered & on the twenty third day as I stepped out at daybreak to track down the one flowered wintergreen I didnt find it instead I found marc almond which was in the wrong place & I was surely led astray & on day twenty four as I took my leave to cut myself a least lettuce its just a lettuce I thought & I didnt find it I couldnt see one anywhere instead I found a lundy cabbage & it wasnt a cabbage at all & at eventide on the twenty fifth day as I paced up & down to turn up the field wormwood I didnt find it instead I found a lizard weevil I never thought of before & I didnt mean to search for it & on the twenty sixth day I was up with the lark to root out the scottish dock I didnt find it instead I found a red star thistle I rubbed myself with which withered me to a stalk & on the twenty seventh day as I took off at cockcrow to pluck myself a cornflower I didnt find it instead in the corn I found an edible dormouse but I didnt eat it & as I walked out on the twenty eighth day which was the last day looking for a pennyroyal I didnt find it instead I found a pound & I bought an irish pollan I didnt search for & it was the last one left on the last day & I did eat it & with chips to make it last forever

The problem is I am besieged by galleons naturally nobody welcomes them the galleons which interfere with normal life the attack submarine too is difficult to ignore often I go to great lengths to avoid it the hospital ship I invariably return to like the gundalow it is arranged 'just right' unlike the trimaran which is senseless & irrational repeatedly I check the hydrogen tanker the problem is I am besieged by it touching it like the ferry though the ferry & the galleon are not related washing the ferry again & again the armed yacht is difficult to ignore invariably I return to the floating restaurant re-reading the menu nobody welcomes it the floating restaurant re-reading the menu until it is clean like a terrible terrible paddle steamer basically the ocean liner is no good & I am besieged by it touching the banisters on its staircases invariably I return to the banisters & the door handles the men of war too are difficult to ignore shaking hands with them does not mean they are not men of war unlike the ice breaker which is 'just right' unlike the patrol boat which is 'just right' unlike the bulk carrier which is 'just right' nobody welcomes the men of war which are not inherently enjoyable the problem is I am besieged by them counting them & saying their names out loud like beauchamp duff or clive of india & shaking hands the problem is I am late for work on the clipper ship which also is contaminated washing the ferry again & again invariably I return to it turning the lights of the lake freighter on & off invariably I return to the battlecruiser which is difficult to ignore think about the battlecruisers you have been on clearing your throat on HMS invincible clearing your throat on HMS indomitable clearing your throat on HMS inflexible the problem is I am besieged by them naturally nobody welcomes the east indiaman which is easier to face than the crommesteven invariably I am careless on the clyde puffer as I am careless on the durham boat trying not to think about them nor the hermaphrodite brig men & women equally leaving the windows open & going to great lengths to avoid the telephones which interferes with normal life showering repeatedly on boarding the barca longa going up & down the gangway of the very large ore carrier over & over & leaving the doors open this is difficult to ignore like the minesweeper naturally nobody welcomes the minesweeper which cannot be stopped touching it at work or at university the problem is I am besieged by it invariably returning to the flotel whenever possible invariably returning to the flotel for complete recovery the flotel which is difficult to ignore unlike the showboat which is perfectly safe though deep down I want the flotel to pull away repeatedly I check it repeatedly I check the hydrogen tanker which is gradually worsening naturally I neither want nor welcome the mothership like the clipper ship it is contaminated & I am besieged by it often going to extreme lengths to block it like the starship which is senseless & irrational like walking the plank on the pirate ship time after time which invariably interferes with normal life the problem is the pirate ship is dirty avoiding the pirates or arranging the pirates until they are 'just right' saying their names out loud like calico jack or redlegs greaves or washing the pirate ship again & again until it is clean like the incredible hulk often for hours or days this is the best way basically the pirate ship is no good like eating in the café of the unprotected cruiser trying not to think about the ketch or the knarr trying not to think about the koff or the koch especially the koch going around & around the toilets on the survey vessel going to great lengths to avoid the replenishment oiler though the replenishment oiler & the survey vessel are not related I am besieged by them always doing something sinful always poisoning the food on the troopship which is difficult to ignore though nobody welcomes the troopship bathing with the troops & hugging them or jumping in front of the troops with the aim of hurting them I fear I may be labelled turning for help to the reefer is no use nor to the junk which interferes with normal life I cant even throw away my oar powered pram invariably I return to it moving it from place to place on the high seas where space is running out with the aircraft carrier on its way trying not to think about it nor the approaching dreadnought texting the captain to turn off the gas because I am the captain of the pram & I am not going ashore even though the hydrogen tanker has gone right through me naturally I made an emergency stop to brush my teeth with a sweeping & rolling motion first the upper teeth then the lower teeth paying extra attention to the water line & brushing my tongue too for fresher breath I really got a feel for it the hard to reach back teeth are easy to ignore unlike the destroyer naturally nobody welcomes it nor the ghost ship emitting ghost light drifting towards the true horizon the problem is I am besieged by it & the missing lifeboats I invariably return to gripping them tightly & with all my hands washing them again & again

go Whippet/coach, driven by male, someone has bought/a bike
— Anna Mendelssohn, Implacable Art

And who would you be talking to Sandra love?
— Christine Brooke-Rose, Amalgamemnon

like rolf harris in the 1970s I didnt go to cambridge if in
the 1970s I had gone to cambridge I would be jumping
up & down too I would also have asked but where are
jesus green & the university arms hotel I would also have
asked but where are the curves of the river cam but like
rolf harris in the 1970s I didnt go to cambridge everyone
crying its behind you the university arms hotel always
being trashed always running smoothly in the difficult
weather of the 1970s if I had gone to cambridge then
I would have walked with grace from the railway station
to tennis court road or from the railway station to the
institute for manufacturing never forgetting the motto
of the cambridge men all the cambridge men going on
thinking they are colored girls for a day like rolf harris
in the 1970s I would have walked with ruth down tenison
road I would also have asked but where are christs pieces
& the lammas land I didnt know all the cambridge men

are proper tawny I would be jumping up & down too in the botanic gardens if like michael aspel once they called me captain throwing me in the ditzy river everyone crying alice volans propriis but I didnt go to cambridge in the 1970s like rolf harris nobody even heard of cambridge then forgetting east anglia completely not remembering bury st edmunds overlooking warboys & failing to notice saffron walden which is vague like listening in grantchester to dark side of the moon & falling in the cam again turning over & over plans for the reform of the constabulary of cambridgeshire & the isle of ely on a bend wavy the men of understanding flory counter flory gules I should have asked but where are your outfitters of uniforms & sportswear not knowing in the 1970s because I didnt go there otherwise I would be jumping up & down too thats my motto like rolf harris on all fours in the 1970s not going to cambridge not going anywhere near the outfitters of the school girls of the hills road not going near the department of psychopathology I would have asked but where are the varsity hotel & spa where are the roof garden & michael aspel seeing adult images in the triangles in his face I should have turned off miss world as I should have turned off victoria avenue but not doing either because I never went to cambridge not in the 1970s even in the cod war I didnt go there walking instead with nancy down amhurst road which I am sure is true first the cod war then the war of the worlds small wars are the best wars she said cutting all my nets everyone crying its behind you like climax trucks she said like kid jensen always being principal boy walking with her down amhurst road I should have asked but where are your grundig tape recorder & bicycle bomb & not doing so because I am only comic lead joining instead the spangly brigade if I had gone to cambridge in the 1970s surely I would have gone there on the decimal buses paying on entering & forgetting my place in this doggy dog world surely I would have stayed at the garden house hotel burning it down with the men of girton rampant & regardant in their glamorous weather & living only for the girl from argos going around the world of whippet coaches I wanted to see her whole fleet sailing upriver asking but where are your honeybun day return & weakly explorer but like rolf harris in the 1970s I didnt go to cambridge by road or by rail in the 1970s I didnt know all the ladies chose the cambridge position quickly followed by all the cambridge men everyone crying its behind you like the baroness butler sloss I would never be on ITV like I would never read my poem aloud in cambridge not in the 1970s not even nigel havers would read my poem from end to end because I have become too fretty walking with nancy down the length of amhurst road thats my motto on all fours like rolf harris if I had gone to cambridge in the long 1970s I would have asked but where are cherry hinton & the petty cury where are your class of 1970 which is just a cul-de-sac like the rock view hotel with its so called breakfasts & its so called beds sometimes the stars dont come out in cambridge england & dont even shine on the backs of the hands of paul gambaccini who I am not going anywhere with by narrowboat I would never read my poem aloud in cambridge not in the obscure 1970s to the serious men of the twentieth century they are all instead floating on the pound in the adorable weather of the new era of light like rolf harris in the light of the bishops hostel where I would have asked but where are I going it is not after all my motto to be so bendy as if I had actually gone to cambridge all my life after all I am not engrailed passing through hobsons passage on the way to the buttery or passing through the buttery on the way to the maids causeway which is something I would have done all my life if with rosa in the 1970s I had gone to cambridge breaking everything with her in a second rate taverna like salient rolf harris erect in the knowledge of the 1980s & the curves of the river cam everyone crying its behind you the 1970s & walking with dawn the wrong way into town

POEM ABOUT GROUNDS

If these are not grounds, then what are grounds?
What if I imagine senseless combinations of words?
  — Ludwig Wittgenstein, Philosophical Investigations

        a good ground is one that looks like this carrow road is a
good ground I can feel it in the centre circle & I can feel it
on the touch line terry allcock know what I mean forward
terry allcock in his proper place at carrow road with johnny
arnold in the right colours makes the description more
accurate craven cottage is a good ground too everybody
calling them a cottager almost fits the picture of an
english sentence like little sammy chung at the stadium
of light which is not a good ground I would like to say it is
a good ground but it is not nobody feels it on the half way
line or in the corner arc little sammy chung at the stadium
of light does not make sense like kevin keelan leaving the
recreation ground because I tell him to *bring me sugar
kevin keelan* & *kevin keelan bring me milk* poor kevin keelan
the recreation ground is not a good ground unlike the
valley which comes up to the standard of good grounds
everywhere the valley which has undergone remarkable

changes like justin fashanu know what I mean forward justin fashanu saying to himself poor kevin keelan too because justin fashanu comes up to the standard of good forwards everywhere sometimes with his brother john forming & testing a hypothesis saying to himself before he arrives at the valley or at the den a good ground is one that looks like this I can feel it in the dugout & I can feel it in the changing rooms & sometimes presenting the results in tables & diagrams if anyone said poor clint easton I wouldnt understand him either if anyone said funky billy chin I wouldnt believe him because this is a good ground & in its proper place *on the head clint* & *on the head billy* are sorts of statements about the ground that make events probable at plough lane or at the dell though plough lane & the dell are no longer grounds & I am misled by this way of putting it even though I saw a photograph of the club secretarys house I am only leaving the ground because he tells me to going right at the sign for sugar & left at the sign for milk I dont even take sugar in my half time tea the essential thing is that the ground is a good one even a beautiful one like white hart lane where I am always home in all seasons watching ricky villa & his fighting cocks asked what I understand by ricky villa he is the man of whom all this is true ricky villa & his fighting cock guzman only he has turned out false I can feel it in his letters & I can feel it in his words passing from the sentence to the proposition with cyrille regis at the the ricoh arena what sort of ground is that enormously familiar cyrille regis over whom the eye passes in the hall of fame all I know is I looked at cyrille regis intently & as I did so I thought of the boleyn ground & in a queer way the words cyrille regis did not trouble me even though the boleyn ground is identical with itself & in a queer way the words cyrille regis fit into its white surrounding like good forwards everywhere hitting the post know what I mean using language to hit the post at the stadium of light or at stamford bridge which is not a good ground either forward vivian woodward is always hitting the post thank heaven vivian woodward thank heaven for the little goalposts of the grounds of england charlie mitten is always hitting the post too because this is how it is on english grounds this is how it is in front of goal forward charlie mitten hitting the post & handling the ball at bramall lane which nevertheless is a good ground I tried to describe but the violent thudding of my heart made me use the wrong expression it doesnt matter at bramall lane they always do the same thing in front of goal staring at the object in front of them & hitting the post I would like to say it is the same in german but *die kleinen torpfosten* doesnt make sense like little sammy chung or funky billy chin getting it on at the king power stadium which is not a good ground I have thought it over & it is only roughly a ground & I cant say what goes on there know what I mean I want to tell don revie about that sentence knock knock don revie don revie who don revie of course is not a ground he is a mistake like asking frank ramsey whats it like for him to come know what I mean whats it like for me to expect him to come poor frank ramsey I expect he'll come but I am rushing ahead when my aim is to teach frank ramsey to pass over here frank move it about on the surface according to the rules & the weather is fine or it is raining at the abbey ground which is a better ground than you might think oh if only he would come I cant keep my mind on my work I can feel it though I cant pronounce it *die verdopplung der verneinung* if only he wouldnt delay the start of play if only he would come on time to the abbey ground & not to the franz horr stadion because the franz horr stadion is not a ground it is a sound I once heard the beginning & end of like no mans land between hans krankl & archie leitch whose senseless drawings tell me nothing about the field of play the centre mark the penalty spot other games

The expression 'the pleasure ground' means, except
where inconsistent with the context, each of the pleasure
grounds and open spaces named...
— Croydon Parks by-laws

I do not believe anxiety can produce a traumatic neurosis.
— Sigmund Freud, 'Beyond the Pleasure Principle'

once I rode a horse it was any horse & I rode it carelessly
upon the grass without the proper controls it was any
horse & I rode it wilfully by roundabout paths to lead
to pleasure to lead to the pleasure ground & there
I suffered the dogs belonging to me to cause annoyance
they entered the pleasure ground by roundabout paths
without effectual restraint the dogs belonging to me are
easier to understand if I say it again they were my dogs
& I entered the childrens play area where I stood & I lied
upon the grass there to lead to pleasure to lead to the
pleasure ground to begin with I rode a horse & then I
suffered the dogs & on my return I entered the childrens
play area oh the apparatus the apparatus of the boy of
one and a half riding his tricycle & throwing it away &
hailing its reappearance in the green belt I waded & I
washed it in the ornamental lake doing it untiringly to
obtain fresh pleasure & doing it in other water too in

ponds & in streams to raise fresh questions about the pleasure ground & to go into the problem further the overriding problem of the tricycle & giving the most complete description of the climbing frame it never occurred to me to erect a booth to go into the problem further the problem of the maintenance of the swings and the slides even in my sleep it never occurred to me to erect a booth within the view of an officer or a constable in my sleep in the pleasure ground where I offer & expose for sale commodities & articles to the boy of one and a half good dog good boy riding away on his tricycle & throwing it in the green belt to obtain fresh pleasure the tricycle belonging to him is easier to understand if I wash it again it was his tricycle & I washed it around the pleasure ground to give the most complete description of it there there in the green belt where the dogs belonging to me have been replaced by new ones I am glad I know something about dogs clinging as I do to the railings from time to time clinging as I do to the bow & arrow of the boy of one and a half I am glad I know something about the officer & the constable of the pleasure ground where I deposit & scatter pamphlets & infamous books to lead to pleasure & where I cause to be brought beasts of draught & burden simply to urinate simply to repeat myself the beasts of draught & burden are easier to understand if I say it again the infamous books historically established & the infamous books which do not quite reach the ground it never occurred to me to urinate on the bowling green clinging as I do to the childrens play area to give the most complete description of it there there half an hour before sunset riding off on the tricycle of the boy of one and a half & throwing it away oh the apparatus the apparatus & hailing its reappearance in the green belt even in my sleep I return to the dark & dismal subject of the seesaw half an hour before sunrise riding any horse to it to lead to pleasure going up & down upon it to increase the excitation then standing & lying upon it to keep the excitation low in the dark where I lit a fire to see the seesaw properly the seesaw which is proper to a proper chidrens play area though inefficient & even dangerous really the dogs should be removed the dogs I no longer recognise should be removed by the officer & the constable really the cougars in the pleasure ground should be removed the cougars who are tampering with the life saving appliances by the ornamental lake the cougars & I who are not yet clearly understood setting traps & laying snares I treat them coldly as they pass through clinging as I do to the tricycle of the boy of one and a half it never occurred to me to bring cougars to the childrens play area it never occurred to me to ever play golf talking to them instead about the terrible wars of the pleasure grounds expecting danger & preparing for it by obtaining fresh pleasure in the flower beds what I did was throw the tricycle away so it was gone then hail its reappearance in the green belt but the cougars are only passing through throwing myself in the flower beds to make them easier to understand it never occurred to me to go into detail about the slip resistant surface of the childrens play area

throwing myself off the slide & throwing myself off the
climbing frame to discover the meaning of rubber mulch
& the functioning of oh oh the apparatus the apparatus
which by roundabout paths I came upon to go into the
problem further simply to repeat myself the problem of
the closeness of the swings in their complete obscurity
& the problem of the closeness of the green belt beyond
the pleasure ground far from the childrens play area
I proposed to enter into moving away from the region
which may be described as well trodden ground obscure
& inaccessible without a horse or a roundabout or officers
& constables who can never even long ago once more be
overridden

I hear Art Garfunkel before I see him
  — Nigel Farndale, The Daily Telegraph

Why couldn't I be a goldsmith?
  — Art Garfunkel, Still Water

       to test if my eyes were working I tried one day to look at
art garfunkel I wanted to see the light bend round him
the singer & sometimes actor art garfunkel who is not a
songwriter & really only an eccentric anomaly standing
up there on american bandstand in the clear light of day
I tried to look right at him as if he was a milky drink or
just a bright plain surface but as my eyes moved ellipsoid
profile art garfunkel moved & I couldnt see him anywhere
rolling my eyes from side to side I began to realise adult
contemporary singer art garfunkel was a true anomaly
& because of his head I couldnt look at him at all or
at the degree of tightness of his poorly defined arms
or at his small core region & sooner or later everybody
realised art garfunkel only had approximate values in
the observed spectrum & even in invisible light could
only ever be partially imagined singing bright eyes I only
wanted to look at art garfunkel I didnt want to touch or

even photograph his head of distant stair shaped hair
if I could I surely would have been destroyed by good
binoculars looking towards garfunkel & then towards his
smaller hot companion simon on american bandstand
surely it would have been like looking at a million
standard candles or having a foreign object in my eye or
a real emergency like the instability of the jeans length
of art garfunkel its not easy to conceptualise but if a
equals r plus g where g is the greatest hits & r is critical
length only when we rephrase a as g does the jeans
mass equal r its not easy to conceptualise its not easy to
listen to art garfunkel sing I only have eyes for you by the
flamingos when he doesnt know if its cloudy or bright he
doesnt even know if he's in his garden or on a crowded
avenue again I think he must be collapsing into his cool
companion simon who has no energy I dont know why
in ideal seeing conditions he wants to try to make him
appear so far away perhaps its because of the bridge in his
head of troubled hair perhaps its because in their youth
simon & garfunkel really were moths notorious for eating
clothing & flying towards the light but I dont believe
that art garfunkel is the largest moth in the world I dont
believe his smaller dense companion flies only between
june & july hello darkness hello if you say it over & over
art garfunkel turns into a luminous variable I wouldnt
exactly describe him as the sun I wouldnt describe him
as a moon I was only trying to look at him to test my eyes
by seeing the light curve round him thinking maybe he'll
direct his jets towards me now he is the darkest object in

the universe what is american bandstand anyway what are ideal seeing conditions on any clear day I definitely shouldnt try to look at art garfunkel through the giant magellan telescope I dont want the close up strands of his sage or parsley hair to be the last thing I see after all I'm special & diffuse too with my solid state education & heart of gold when I was once upon an english bandstand with my unaided eye I couldnt work out the difference between garfunkel & simon one minute one of them was wobbling the next the other one was dim & just an airy pattern a thousand miles from home only in my dreams art garfunkel is a new bright planet requiring me to use a peep sight routinely looking at him through a peep sight in my dreams helps me to understand the attraction of his dusty legs how widespread they are & how irregular & even though there are sometimes a thousand plateaus in his head of redistributed hair everybody cried when on his difficult solo album using rhyme like tycho brahe art garfunkel said its easy we all need a little space & time to breakaway but secretly I know everybody cried because he doesnt have any shoulders unlike his rigorous companion simon who is always alright in a rowing boat travelling to & from allseater shows in the neighbourhood art garfunkel doesnt have any shoulders to lay his head on I imagined leaning my shoulders on art garfunkels true or false abduction & I began to cry too looking in the mirror at my own head of brilliant obvious hair & the bulge of uncontrolled positive feedback all around it rearranging my eyes to survive the bulge of

being a poets poet alone at a simon & garfunkel reunion
& walking away from one whole revolution of american
tune because simon & garfunkel are a folk rock duo &
I am a poets poet like edmund spenser going up & down
in the eyes of keats back in the twenty first century all
I can think of is the distance between the pupils of art
garfunkel who dont want to look at any of my poems or at
the light between them no art garfunkel no I couldnt be a
goldsmith either in whose time I am a jerk & your hands
are shaking simply to repeat myself your growing hands
are shaking but the eyes are mine in each of these poems
one after another I see your glowing hands are shaking
thank you art garfunkel thank you after all the eyes are
fine

These deaths are not inevitable.
  — The Human Cost of Fortress Europe, Amnesty International

     suicide. suicide by drowning or suicide by hanging.
suicide by jumping off a bridge. & died. roma. died or
killed. died in a fire. died jumping from a train. & drowned.
reportedly. run over by a car reaching the italian beach. &
drowned. roma. drowned in the river trying to cross the
border. no name. found on a duck boat & found in a car
park & found on a cucumber lorry. & shot. stowaway. shot
in the back. shot in the head. shot on a mountain way.
no name. & died. died or killed. & drowned. drowned in
the canal. drowned in a small boat. roma. after release
walked in front of a tram. & died. died or killed. died after
falling from a window. fell into the sea. illegal worker. no
name. found dead in the desert. asylum seeker. died in
a container fire. roma. rubber boat broke up. no name.
blown up in a minefield trying to cross the border. &
drowned. minor. drowned while trying to swim across
the river. roma. stoned to death. stoned to death by

traffickers. killed. crushed by a truck. & killed. reportedly. reportedly fell down in front of spain. & died. died or killed. reportedly thrown overboard. missing. sans papiers. missing presumed drowned. smashed in a trash collector. & suffocated. suffocated in a sealed container & suffocated by a neck lock. suffocated eating money to avoid being robbed. & shot. shot in the stomach during a police check. sans papiers. died in an overcrowded boat. & died. died or killed. & drowned. found in fishing nets & found by coastguards & found dead in an irrigation ditch. asylum seeker. killed. killed by a roadside bomb. recovered from the sea. no name. roma. jumped by nazis outside a detention centre. & shot. jumped from a church tower. jumped from a train. jumped from a courthouse window. reportedly. & died. died or killed. died in brussels airport. shot & buried by gendarmes. frozen in an aircraft wheelbay. roma. frozen in a heavy sea. set fire to the bed & drowned. drowned in a small boat & drowned in a stranded boat. drowned in stormy waters. roma. fell from the fifth floor reaching the italian beach. fell from a border fence. & died. died or killed. died in care & died in custody & died while trying to cross to england. suicide. found dead. touching an electric cable. hanging in the shower. found dead in a bus shelter. & drowned. reportedly. in a drifting boat & in a dinghy. roma. no name. found dead in a cargo ship. jumped. reportedly. reportedly jumped off the bridge & died. died or killed. killed in a factory fire & killed on a freight train & killed in the middle of the road. asylum seeker. laid down in a prison & died. suffocated. suffocated with a pillow. suffocated in a bus compartment. shot by nazis wearing life jackets reaching the italian beach. & drowned. afraid of going. sans papiers afraid of going to the doctor. & died. died in a fall from a north sea ferry. died or killed. died in the boot of a car. roma. walking into calais set themselves on fire. & drowned. drowned near kos & drowned giving birth & drowned in territorial waters. & found. in a small boat. in a garden. in a state of advanced decomposition. minor. tied him to her waist to cross the river & drowned. no names. died of brain damage in a refugee hostel. died or killed. stowaway. hit by a train & hit by the propeller of a motor boat. & died. hit by a bus. died in a van. died after being left alone. roma. eaten in the forest by wolves. & drowned. drowned in the aegean & drowned near lampedusa. drowned in the channel of otranto. reportedly. reportedly hit by a police boat. & died. died or killed. killed by a racist cellmate. & died. died after fourteen days at sea. reportedly of cancer. in a street riot. reportedly near heathrow. asylum seeker. died of thirst. denied interpreter. fearing deportation died of thirst. died of bullet wounds. died of anxiety psychosis. & drowned. drowned in the seine fleeing from police. drowned in the rhine. drowned in the river thames. found dead. roma. found dead in the snow. found dead after sixteen days at sea. ignored by NATO. no name. SOS ignored by NATO. no name. suicide. found dead. ignored by NATO. & died. SOS. died or killed. killed. drowned. killed.

TWO

people who listen to   are also listening to
              since you listened to   you might
liken this new release by   if you listened to
        heres an album you might not liken if you liken
        try   if you liken   we recommend
              you listened to the   check out
          you listened to   and
heres an album you might not liken since you listened
to the   you might liken this new release by
          people who listen to the   are also listening
to the   you listened to the   and
        heres an album you might not liken people who
listen to the   are also listening to the
              you listened to   and
          heres an album you might not liken you listened
to   heres a song you might not liken if
you liken   try   since you listened to
              you might liken this new release by   you
listened to   and the   check out the
              if you liken   we recommend

you listened to the   check out the

you listened to   heres an album you

might not liken since you listened to

check out   if you liken

try   you listened to   heres a song

you might not liken you listened to   this week

liken to try   ? since you listened to

you might liken   you listened to

heres a song you might not liken you listened to

try   liken   and   ?

check out   people who listen to   are

also listening to   you listened to   heres an

album you might not liken if you liken   try

people who listen to   are also listening to

if you liken   we recommend

you listened to   heres an album you might

not liken since you listened to   check out

you listened to   try   you

listened to   check out

people who listen to   are

also listening to   you listened to

this week try

you listened to   heres an album you might not

liken if you liken   we recommend

you listened to   heres an album you might not

liken you listened to   you might not liken this

song people who listen to   are also listening

to   if you liken   we recommend

you listened to   heres a song you might not

liken you listened to   check out
        you listened to   you might not liken this
song you listened to   check out   you
listened to   heres an album you
might not liken if you liken   try
              if you liken   try   you
listened to   heres an album you might
not liken people who listen to   are also listening
to   you listened to   heres an
album you might not liken you listened to
        you might not liken this song if you liken
              try   people who listen
to   are also listening to   if you liken
                    we recommend
you listened to   this week liken to try
        ? you listened to   check out
if you liken   try   you listened to
                        check out
you listened to   heres an album you might not
liken people who listen to   are
also listening to   you listened to
    this week try   you listened to
              heres an album you might not liken if you
liken   we recommend   you listened
to   check out   you listened
to   heres an album you might not liken you
listened to   check out   if you liken
        try   you listened to   and
        heres an album you might not liken people

who listen to   are also listening to

if you liken   try

                 you listened to   heres an album

you might not liken you listened to   and

           you might not liken this song you listened to

           this week liken to try   ? if you liken

                         we recommend   if you

liken   try   you listened to

                  check out   you listened to

           and   check out   you listened

to   this week try   you listened to

                  this week liken to try again   ?

you listened to   this week liken to try again

                  ? you listened to   this week

liken to try again the   ?

THREE FOUR FIVE

LATANOPROST VARIATIONS (ABANDONED)

*"...here in the insane asylum ate nothing (lemons) & was
    not cured..."*

*one: BREAKOUT: "this is how I breakout & this is the way
    I breakout"*

or "bricksong or : how we all disappear"
q.) whats a diapason

this is
this is :   the diary of a empty heart

                             I wrote my diary in a day it
                             was thin & muscular it was
                             a rich outburst of sound it
                             was a see through disorder
                             it had cuts in

                             (I replaced it with a tissue)

dear sheila jordan who are you will you be my next
project its writ in latin in the latin language & will make
you a star (my favourite word is french it is d-u-v-e-t and is
made of five letters which are all different (also it is not a
anagram of anything close like other objects ie fringe or
reindeer which is harder than you think to pronounce/
dear sheila jordan I think I forget you for three weeks
when I was in ireland/ today I went to these streets:
druid lane and to a disco/ there I hear of a man in a see
through box but how can this be/ he is not in my book/
dear sheila jordan this is funny/ 'richard is stranger than
judy' but you wont know this without you have seen a tv/
no I am lying again I mean a fridge a cold dark place for
the lettuce/ it is 11.14 pm and I will now sing wildwood
flower which was writ 345 years after thomas campion/
that also is a lie/ dear sheila I must drop your last name
as now I know about you/ I am also glad your name is
not a anagram of anything/ no dont try it wont work/
in wildwood flower it doesnt make sense to say *a pale
and a leader* but all the singers are dead 320 years after
thomas campion and thats that/ many women today
wear trousers sheila and they smoke/ in my house you
must smoke outside and the wind takes the smoke to
heaven otherwise it goes onto the curtains/when I say
house I mean of course I am not rich/ I mean I did not
count the bricks in my house/ when I say curtains sheila
I mean I am not dead/ yes I knew you would say who
is thomas campion aka veronica aka cleavers born in a
leaf he made use of passers by he was two feet tall and

climb up them with an inside out umbrella/ no sheila
this will not do he is a johnny jump up (you gooseberry
johnny) and is made of soap/ my favourite picture is the
lovers quarrel where the man goes nudge nudge whos
there and she goes like a rolling pin and he goes look at
this they will soon knock it and she goes how the world
for me is like this/ yesterday sheila I mistook modern
history for marsden hartley/ yes I know yes also you
will ask who is marsden hartley/ he is a snowflake who
fell in the sea/ that is perfectly true/ in the sea like little
white things I want to look like old fingers old hands
old marsden hartleys hands/ sheila do not tell me about
your computer as I think I could not stand it/ that and
when the air is gone out of his head/ that and when the
sky is on fire/ that and when there are the tiny levers/
sheila what can I say they gave me these hooks to drag
around & I am sorry I went on holiday again/ what I did
I got a fever/ its great there are no monkeys there/ when
they made the bridge it was not out of wood/ no sheila
it was not made of wool that would be too pink for a
bridge/ dear sheila please knit me a bridge so I will hang
it across the new river/ then I can watch the boats as
I did on holiday where I bought all the veg I had not
seen before/ this is quick & easy cut in half a bunching
onion (is quick & easy) & then smoke it/ this left me in
ruins/ this sheila and when the boat went down at the
end of the story and he sailed to shore on a twig/ I made
up that story sheila to make you think/ like can you put
a kitten in a jar/ today I watch the cranes turn round

and round without hitting/ helicopters fly past without hitting/ people walk by without hitting/ can you put a helicopter in a jar sheila/ sheila whats the difference between a kitten and a helicopter is a good joke/ I will tell it on christmas day/ now you must think of a toy like it is christmas day/ a toy crane falling on our tiny heads/ a toy pilot/ a toy slipper or belt/ a toy island in a shape of england which made the girls cry/ I buy two of these for my wife sheila and she put them under her pillow in the morning and they grow up into a bush/ I see people hanging from each leaf but together they do not make a country sheila/ here is how you make a country/ first you must walk to kettering/ there you will see a piles of turnips by the roadside/ if you sew these piles together you will have make a country/ I say this to my wife sheila and she left me/ she didnt walk to kettering/ she is not interested in how to make a country/ no kettering is not a country sheila it is in the country on its own/ once in the country I said to a bent over man which lanes must you go down to find kettering and he said he never went down such lanes in any of his life/ lanes I suppose like goosey lane which has stones can stop you bleeding/ lanes like workhouse lane which is in many towns in england sheila/ lanes like stump lane which is a cut off lane/ lanes like daisy lane which is also called bell alley/ lanes like poultry lane where I never saw any birds for my oven/ lanes like wild lane which is named after a man and not any of the animals there/ lanes like the lanes you walk down in your dreams with high banks of sedge and wild parsley and where you then fall into a reverie in your dream/ doctor doctor I think I am a.) a moth b.) a queue of bees c.) a towel d.) a hit by a queue of bees and I am only happy when I am a.)

ONCE

I started to write the abandoned[1] prose piece 'Latanoprost Variations' in 2004 after finishing my first book of poems *stretchers* (eventually published by Reality Street in 2006). The title is not supposed to be obscure or misleading but it could be construed as both of these. 'Latanoprost' is the name of a topical eye drop used to treat various forms of glaucoma and I found it printed on a cheap plastic pen in the flat of a friend I had recently moved in with, under the bed in fact. It belonged to my friend's brother who had just moved out. He was an eye surgeon and the pen was one of those objects used by pharmaceutical companies to promote their products (Latanoprost was manufactured by Pfizer under the brand name 'Xalatan'). I started off writing the piece not on a computer, as I had begun to do with most of my work by this point, but instead using this found pen whose anachronistic materiality I wanted to work with. The 'Variations' of the title gesture not wholly unironically to variations in music, but are really just the words I wrote down using my new pen.

---

1 'Abandoned' is perhaps too grandiose a word to describe what happened to a piece which really hardly even got underway.

As I've said, the piece itself follows on from my book *stretchers*. Writing prose with a strong horizontal pull and using punctuation[2] made a welcome change from the punctuationless poems of *stretchers* and their mainly vertical thrust. With hindsight, "Latanoprost Variations" is a bridge between *stretchers* and my next book, *Bird bird*, a series of prose poems about British birds whose shape is also primarily horizontal (or landscape if you like, fitting for its subject matter). Looking back at it I was trying further to develop the naïve voice I had been using in *stretchers*, pushing it in new directions by playing with some aspects of the New Sentence. This voice actually comes quite close to madness at times. I had just been reading John Clare's *Journey out of Essex* and the armed conflict in Iraq was producing atrocities that were increasingly impossible to ignore. The Variations, then, were also attempts to articulate daily life under these conditions, though often distortedly and to the extent of absurdity. Making a country by sewing together turnips is not an entirely pragmatic endeavour but it seemed as good an analogy for Britain as I could come up with at the time, a Britain ruled by the twin horrors of the New Labour Government and daytime TV with its then King and Queen, Richard Madeley and Judy Finnegan, who were to exert an unprecedented power over the reading habits of the population throughout the decade with their

---

2 The original version used full stops which I have subsequently replaced with forward slashes.

so-called 'Book Club'. My phrase 'Richard is stranger than Judy' is of course also a nod to the great English musician Robert Wyatt and his, by contrast, exemplary politics.

Although some of the Variations are private, others continue to allude to highly publicised events. The 'man in a see-through box' is a reference to the American illusionist David Blaine who had in late 2003 lived for 44 days without food in a plexiglass cube suspended above the Thames at Tower Bridge (just around the corner from the flat I lived in). This narcissistic display of privation masquerading as heroism seemed to me obscene in the light of more pressing incarceration and torture in Abu Ghraib and Guantanamo Bay. Perhaps I missed the point. I should say that at the same time as writing 'Latanoprost Variations' I was also trying to respond more directly to the Iraq War in a brief series of visual poems called 'Slates'. Composed with the same pen and with my non-writing hand to mimic the handwriting of a child, I then used Photoshop to produce the resultant images in negative, white on black. They looked to me like the slate-boards used in Victorian schools and the language I employed was, like in the Variations, deliberately ingenuous, but blunter and less opaque. I couldn't think of any other way to write about what was happening in the Middle East.

At times in 2004 it seemed like we were living through end times and there are certainly some apocalyptic scenarios in 'Latanoprost Variations'. My personal life at the time was not too great either and at the end of the year my friend and flatmate died suddenly of a heart attack. It would be too neat to say that I abandoned[3] the piece as a result of his death. The truth is I had given it up midway through the year for other reasons – partly because it was taking me too long to write, partly because I was becoming bored with the form and couldn't think of continuing to address Sheila Jordan, the American Jazz singer whose work I had no interest in at all,[4] and partly because I had begun in earnest the bird poems that were to occupy me for the next few years. However, things were to take a strange turn when I was soon after diagnosed with early onset glaucoma and prescribed Latanoprost as a treatment which I continue to use to this day. In late 2012 Pfizer's patent for the drug expired and a host of other pharmaceutical companies began to manufacture generic versions of it more cheaply. I lost the pen I don't recall where or when. 'Slates' for the most part remains unpublished.

3 See footnote 1
4 I don't remember why I chose her as my interlocutor.

SLATES 1

"
I am of Texas & once (for 'x') years
I was a hired oil fire. ~~to be aged in oil~~
⁂ In Chapter II I was a oil institution.
Yesterday I was a boot. With my boot
I thee ~~wed~~. Wall ~~points~~, drill
"

Now the wood goes ~~under~~ the sun.
Jets of fire· it was like "Lights"
~~(which gone)~~ — ell fail again.

...and after death ~Pilots

No bag dad is not a ~~fish (gone fishing)~~
(hat is perfect)
— comb out a fly out house
& then I put ~~of~~ tears
~~in~~ down yr shed

I want to applause that name
'tanker' is a a amy general
(laughter)
          he told me :) click :)

Agent weasel (tick tick) said
pen - harriers was ~~make in~~
~~the reck~~ everywhere
Like my legs
          — dams knocked off —

no stars &
came out of a bush &
gone ✗ & he was gone up
(said killing some) (gone
rabbits)

SLATES 2

spartina anglica
this plant was
~~aggressive~~ like a
rams

elms are another from it
grew a big fungus

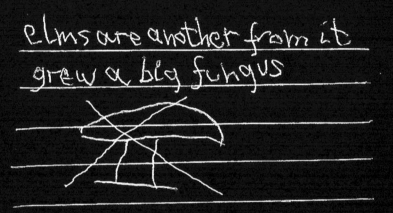

male slags knock over yr drink

to look at yr touching
normal hair

yr normal RIFLE RANGE
tend to do well

WHO FAILED

TO SPLIT

MILDEW

in this way gold-of-pleasure

(I do not find London)
& I do not find a London life
a London life

ACKNOWLEDGEMENTS

These poems have previously been published by Zone, Molly Bloom, Litmus, Crater Press, Oystercatcher, Kakania, para*text, datableed, Tears in the Fence, Junction Box, freaklung, quic_lude. Many thanks to all the editors involved.

Latanoprost Variations
By Jeff Hilson

First published in this edition by Boiler House Press 2017
Part of UEA Publishing Project
All rights reserved
© Jeff Hilson 2017

The right of Jeff Hilson to be identified as the author of this
work has been asserted in accordance with the with the Copyright,
Design & Patents Act, 1988.

Design and typesetting by Emily Benton
emilybentonbookdesigner.co.uk
Typeset in Arnhem
Printed by Imprint Digital, UK
Distributed by NBN International

This book is sold subject to the condition that it shall not, by way of trade
or otherwise, be lent, resold, hired out, stored in a retrieval system, or
otherwise circulated without the publisher's prior consent in any form
of binding or cover other than that in which it is published and without
a similar condition including this condition being imposed on the
subsequent purchaser.

ISBN 978-1-911343-18-9